D1716309

Searchlight
BOOKS™

Climate Change

Climate Change and

Rising Temperatures

Kevin Kurtz

Lerner Publications ◆ Minneapolis

To Adam, Noah, and all the other kids
whose future we adults are responsible for

Copyright © 2019 by Lerner Publishing Group, Inc.

All rights reserved. International copyright secured. No part of this book may be
reproduced, stored in a retrieval system, or transmitted in any form or by any means—
electronic, mechanical, photocopying, recording, or otherwise—without the prior written
permission of Lerner Publishing Group, Inc., except for the inclusion of brief quotations
in an acknowledged review.

Lerner Publications Company
A division of Lerner Publishing Group, Inc.
241 First Avenue North
Minneapolis, MN 55401 USA

For reading levels and more information, look up this title
at www.lernerbooks.com.

Main body text set in Adrianna Regular 14/20.
Typeface provided by Chank.

Library of Congress Cataloging-in-Publication Data

Names: Kurtz, Kevin, author.
Title: Climate change and rising temperatures / Kevin Kurtz.
Description: Minneapolis : Lerner Publications, [2019] | Series: Searchlight books.
    Climate change | Audience: Ages 8–11. | Audience: Grades 4 to 6. | Includes
    bibliographical references and index.
Identifiers: LCCN 2018004443 | ISBN 9781541538627 (lb : alk. paper)
Subjects: LCSH: Climatic changes—Juvenile literature. | Global warming—Juvenile
    literature. | Global environmental change—Juvenile literature. | Nature—Effect of
    human beings on—Juvenile literature.
Classification: LCC QC903.15 .K87 2019 | DDC 551.6—dc23

LC record available at https://lccn.loc.gov/2018004443

Manufactured in the United States of America
1 - 45045 - 35872 - 4/24/2018

Contents

Chapter 1

WHAT IS CLIMATE CHANGE?

If you say, "It was sunny this morning, but it rained this afternoon," you aren't talking about climate. You're talking about weather. Weather is whatever is happening in the air outside. Types of weather include clouds, wind, snow, air temperature, and rain.

Climate is related to weather, but it can't be observed in the same way weather can. To observe climate, scientists must study weather in an area over decades. They look for trends and calculate averages.

Hail is a type of weather. Climate change can affect weather, but climate and weather are two different things.

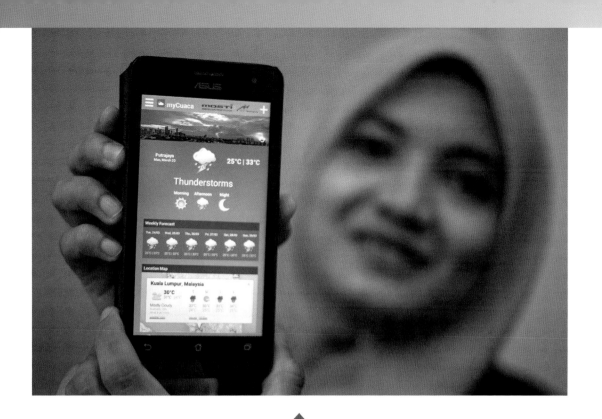

MOST APPS AND TV FORECASTS GIVE INFORMATION ABOUT WEATHER, NOT CLIMATE.

You can think of climate as a menu. It shows the weather options that are most likely to happen in a place. In a desert area, for instance, the weather is likely to be hot and dry.

Weather is the daily special: "Today we are having rain with a side of strong winds." Weather is what actually happens each day.

Temperatures are rising in Antarctica. This is an example of climate change.

A place may have a weather "daily special" that is not on its climate menu. It may have record-breaking cold temperatures or rainfall amounts. If this unusual weather is rare, it will not change the climate menu.

If unusual weather keeps happening, it becomes the new normal weather. Then climate change has occurred.

Mercury's Rising

We are living in a time when climate is changing. Starting in 1880, scientists could look at temperatures from around the world. They figured out the average temperature for the entire planet for that year. They have done this for every year since.

The temperatures from the 1880s are different from recent temperatures. The twenty hottest years on record have all happened since 1995. The five hottest years have all happened since 2010. So the world is getting warmer.

Dry, cracked soil where plants cannot grow can be a symptom of global warming.

Chapter 2

HOTTER ALL THE TIME

Earth wouldn't be as warm as it is if it were not for its atmosphere. Certain gases in Earth's atmosphere trap the sun's heat after it warms the ground. These gases are greenhouse gases.

Greenhouse gases are like a sweater around Earth. A sweater feels warm because it traps heat from your body. Greenhouse gases trap heat rising from the ground. Without them, the average temperature on Earth would be just 0°F (-18°C).

> Greenhouse gases are named after greenhouses. These structures have big glass roofs that let in the sun's light and then trap heat to help plants grow.

STEM In Depth: The Atmosphere's Gases

Only some gases in the atmosphere are greenhouse gases. Most of them are not. In fact, more than 99.9 percent of them aren't greenhouse gases!

Nitrogen is the most abundant non-greenhouse gas. It makes up 78.1 percent of the atmosphere. Oxygen is the next most abundant. It makes up 20.9 percent of the atmosphere.

As for greenhouse gases, carbon dioxide is the most abundant. It makes up just 0.04 percent of the atmosphere. Methane comes in next. About 0.0002 percent of our atmosphere consists of methane.

Humans breathe in oxygen. We breathe out carbon dioxide, also called CO_2.

The History of Climate Change

Earth has been much warmer in the past. You could have worn shorts at the North Pole fifty-five million years ago! At other times, Earth was very cold. Ice may have covered the entire planet.

Scientists have studied why climate change happened in the past. They found it depends on carbon dioxide. The more carbon dioxide in the atmosphere, the warmer it gets. A lot more carbon dioxide was in the air when the dinosaurs were alive. It was as if Earth was wearing three sweaters. A lot less carbon dioxide was in the air during the ice ages. It was as if Earth was wearing a T-shirt.

Animals called woolly mammoths graze in this artist's drawing of what the ice age may have looked like.

When exposed to sunlight, trees and plants turn water and carbon dioxide into food. This takes carbon dioxide out of the air.

In the past, the amount of carbon dioxide changed due to natural causes. Huge volcanic eruptions released enormous amounts of carbon dioxide. This made Earth warmer. Plants slowly removed carbon dioxide from the air. This made Earth cooler.

Carbon Dioxide Overload

The amount of carbon dioxide in the air is rising again. It is not because of natural causes. About 250 years ago, people started inventing lots of new machines. The machines needed energy to run. The cheapest way to get energy was to burn fossil fuels. Fossil fuels are the remains of prehistoric plants and plankton. They are full of carbon. When they are burned, the carbon joins with oxygen to make carbon dioxide. This adds extra carbon dioxide to the atmosphere.

Steam-powered trains were one machine that relied on fossil fuels.

THE GASOLINE USED TO POWER MOST CARS AND TRUCKS IS A FOSSIL FUEL.

▼

Today we have even more machines that need fossil fuel energy. These machines add about 40 billion tons (36 billion t) of carbon dioxide into the atmosphere each year. We are putting another sweater on Earth. Temperatures are rising quickly.

Chapter 3

TEMPERATURE AND OUR PLANET

We are having more hot days. That may not sound like a bad thing—although heat waves can be dangerous. But rising temperatures cause other changes too.

Many people enjoy warm, sunny days. Yet that's not the only change rising temperatures bring.

Many neighborhoods were badly flooded when Hurricane Irma hit at least nine US states in 2017.

More Extreme Storms

Extreme storms happen more often as temperatures rise. Heat is a form of energy. The higher the temperature, the more energy is in the atmosphere. All this extra energy gets into storms. This makes hurricanes and other storms more powerful and dangerous.

Forest fire warning signs such as this one near Lake Hughes, California, are becoming increasingly common in the western United States.

More Droughts and Forest Fires

Hot temperatures make water evaporate faster. This causes soils to dry out quickly. Hot temperatures also create large areas of high air pressure. The pressure pushes away moist air. It cannot rain without this moisture. Without rain, a drought can last for years. Droughts cause trees and plants to dry out. Dry plants lead to more forest fires. This is happening in the western and southeastern United States.

Rising Sea Levels

Warmer temperatures add heat to ocean water. The heat expands the water, causing the sea level to rise. Rising temperatures also melt the ice in glaciers. This is happening in places such as Greenland and Antarctica. The melted glacier water flows into the ocean, and sea levels rise. Coastal cities are having more floods because of this. Some small islands in the Pacific Ocean are completely underwater.

Cars drive through flooded streets in Miami, Florida, after a heavy rain.

ADÉLIE PENGUINS RELY ON THEIR COLD
AND ICY CLIMATE TO SURVIVE.

Wildlife Problems

Rising temperatures are changing habitats around the world. Both polar bears in the Artic and Adélie penguins in the Antarctic live on sea ice. Rising temperatures are melting their homes away. Ticks and other parasites keep heading farther north. They can live in places that used to be too cold for them. These parasites are making more animals and people sick.

Chapter 4

SCIENTISTS RESPOND

Scientists are working hard to understand what is causing rising temperatures. They are also figuring out what we can do to fix the problems that come from rising temperatures.

Climatologists do hands-on research involving Earth's climate. They have college degrees in subjects such as climatology, meteorology, and atmospheric science.

STEM In Depth: Climate Change Stinks!

Scientists are studying all the ways we add greenhouse gases to the air. One of the biggest—and grossest—has to do with raising cattle for food.

When cattle eat grass, methane is released in their stomachs. This greenhouse gas is thirty-four times more powerful than carbon dioxide when it comes to warming the air. Cattle release the methane by passing gas and expelling waste. About a billion cattle are doing this every day. They are creating about 15 percent of the greenhouse gases caused by human activity.

THESE WIND TURBINES COLLECT ENERGY FROM THE WIND SO THAT IT CAN BE USED FOR POWER.

Finding Solutions

Scientists and engineers are looking for ways to stop using fossil fuels. They are developing new ways to get energy from wind and the sun. These sources do not produce greenhouse gases.

Some new solar panels are washable and flexible. Clothing manufacturers might one day sew such panels into clothing. Then people could plug their phones and other devices right into their shirts to charge them! Soon we may have invisible solar panels. These could be placed on any window to generate pollution-free electricity.

Traditional solar panels are often square-shaped and made of hard material. They collect energy from the sun.

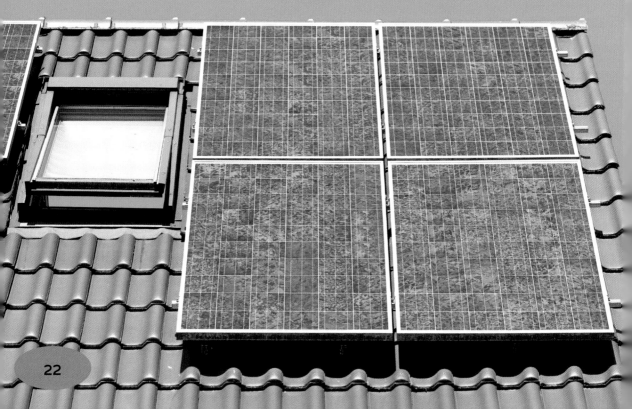

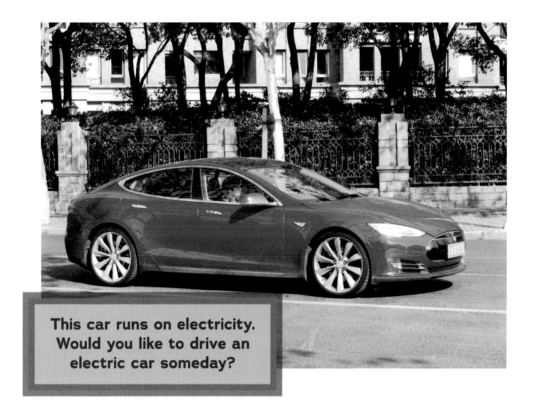

This car runs on electricity. Would you like to drive an electric car someday?

Scientists and engineers are also helping our homes and vehicles use less energy. They have redesigned appliances such as washing machines and refrigerators to use less power. They have figured out ways to build better-insulated homes. This prevents heat and air-conditioning from escaping outside, so we can use less of them. Scientists and engineers have found ways to make powerful electric cars too. If these cars get their electricity from sun or wind power, they can run without producing any greenhouse gases.

Plastic bags are made from fossil fuels.
Many shoppers bring their own bags to
the store as an Earth-friendly alternative.

Scientists and engineers have many ideas to help us. But none of these ideas alone will solve the problems of rising temperatures. It will take all of our help to make a difference.

A Global Solution

Climate change is a big problem, but we have solved big problems before. In the 1980s, scientists found a hole in the ozone layer. Ozone is a gas that surrounds Earth. It blocks harmful radiation from the sun. Too much of this radiation is very bad for humans and animals. It's a danger to every living thing on Earth.

Too much radiation from the sun can cause health conditions such as skin cancer and cataracts, a clouding of the eye's lens.

Household products such as hair spray used to come in aerosol cans that released ozone-harming chemicals. These days, these products are made in a more Earth-friendly way.

The scientists realized that pollution caused the hole. Chemicals from aerosol cans and refrigerators were eating away the ozone. In 1987, countries around the world agreed to ban these chemicals. Since then, the hole in the ozone layer has begun to heal itself. This action prevented a global crisis.

The hole in the ozone was not causing climate change. But its story shows people can work together to solve a global problem. These days, people around the world are coming together to fight climate change. Almost every country has agreed to start reducing the amount of greenhouse gases it produces. Many people are doing this in their homes and businesses. You can help too! Turn off the lights when you're not using them. Walk or bike instead of driving when you can. We can all do our part to help planet Earth.

Biking to nearby places instead of driving helps cut down on fossil fuel use.

What You Can Do

Here are more ideas you can try to help save energy and reduce greenhouse gases:

- **Don't take more food than you can eat.** You can go back for seconds later if you want more! It takes a lot of energy to grow, ship, refrigerate, and cook food. And people in the United States throw away 120 billion pounds (54 billion kg) of food each year.

- **Eat more vegetables.** Cattle create greenhouse gases. It also takes more energy to raise livestock than it does to grow vegetables. If your family buys less meat and more vegetables, it will help reduce greenhouse gases.

- **Replace old light bulbs in your home with LED bulbs.** If a light bulb is warm, it is wasting energy. LED bulbs make light without much heat. They use a lot less energy than older bulbs.

- **Email your elected officials about climate change.** Tell them to make Earth-friendly decisions. Find out how to contact them at https://www.usa.gov/elected-officials.

Climate Change Timeline

1765 James Watt comes up with an idea to redesign and improve the steam engine. This helps kick-start the Industrial Revolution and the high demand for fossil fuels.

1856 The scientist Eunice Foote discovers carbon dioxide is a greenhouse gas.

1980 The scientist Carl Sagan warns the public in his popular book *Cosmos* about the dangers of climate change.

2013 The amount of carbon dioxide in the atmosphere goes over four hundred parts per million. This is the first time it goes that high in human history.

2016 Earth experiences the hottest year on record.

2017 Earth experiences the second-hottest year on record. Almost every country on Earth agrees to sign the Paris Agreement on climate change to reduce their greenhouse gas emissions.

Glossary

atmosphere: the layer of air that surrounds Earth

carbon dioxide: the most abundant greenhouse gas in Earth's atmosphere

climate: the typical weather for an area

drought: a long dry period when an area does not receive enough rain

engineer: a person whose job is to use science and math to figure out the best way to build and invent new things

evaporate: when heat causes liquid to turn into gas

greenhouse gas: a type of gas in the atmosphere that can trap heat from the sun

ice age: a period in the past when Earth was much colder

methane: a greenhouse gas that is thirty-four times stronger at warming the air than carbon dioxide

plankton: things that live in water but are not good swimmers. Most plankton are microscopic.

weather: what the atmosphere does from moment to moment. Weather includes rain, clouds, temperature, and wind.

Learn More about Rising Temperatures

Books

Buchanan, Shelly. *Global Warming*. Huntington Beach, CA: Teacher Created Materials, 2016. Read more about the causes and effects of rising temperatures.

Rowell, Rebecca. *Weather and Climate through Infographics*. Minneapolis: Lerner Publications, 2014. Informational art and interesting text make for a fun read about climate and weather.

Shea, Nicole. *Animals and Climate Change*. New York: Gareth Stevens, 2014. Find out how climate change impacts animal life.

Websites

American Museum of Natural History: Climate Change
https://www.amnh.org/explore/ology/climate-change
Solve fun puzzles, get tips on living green, and learn more at this site.

NASA: Climate Kids
https://climatekids.nasa.gov/
Explore topics such as weather and climate, atmosphere, and energy.

National Geographic Kids: What Is Climate Change?
https://www.natgeokids.com/au/discover/geography/general
-geography/what-is-climate-change/#!/register
Read an informative article on climate change.

Index

Photo Acknowledgments

Image credits: alexeys/iStock/Getty Images, p. 4; Ahmad Yusni/NurPhoto/Getty Images, p. 5; Ashley Cooper/Corbis Documentary/Getty Images, p. 6; Edwin Remsberg/Photographer's Choice/Getty Images, p. 7; DutchScener/iStock /Getty Images, p. 8; Thatchai Wanitchakun/Shutterstock .com, p. 9; AuntSpray/Shutterstock.com, p. 10; Peter Schickert/age fotostock/Getty Images, p. 11; Antonio Pasciucco/iStock/Getty Images, p. 12; Bernard/imageBROKER/Getty Images, p. 13; LightField Studios/Shutterstock.com, p. 14; Carolyn Cole/Los Angeles Times/Getty Images, p. 15; Joseph Sohm/Shutterstock.com, p. 16; FashionStock.com/Shutterstock.com, p. 17; KeithSzafranski/ E+/Getty Images, p. 18; FrameStockFootages/Shutterstock.com, p. 19; emholk/iStock/Getty Images, p. 20; Warren Gretz/Department of Energy/National Renewable Energy Laboratory, p. 21; Jan-Otto/iStock/Getty Images, p. 22; hans-johnson/Flickr (CC BY-ND 2.0), p. 23; David McNew/ Getty Images, p. 24; Roman Sakhno/Shutterstock.com, p. 25; shorrocks/E+/Getty Images, p. 26; Ariel Skelley/DigitalVision/Getty Images, p. 27.

Cover: Tui De Roy/ Minden Pictures/Getty Images.